LEARN THE VALUE OF

Sharing

by Elaine P. Goley

Illustrated by Debbie Crocker

ROURKE ENTERPRISES, INC.
VERO BEACH, FL 32964

© 1989 Rourke Enterprises, Inc.

All rights reserved. No part of this book may be reproduced or utilized in any form or by any means, electronic or mechanical including photocopying, recording or by any information storage and retrieval system without permission in writing from the publisher.

Library of Congress Cataloging-in-Publication Data

Goley, Elaine P., 1949–
   Learning the value of sharing.

   Summary: Suggests ways to enjoy the happiness we can get from sharing, such as making popcorn for the whole family and taking turns using the tennis racket.
   1. Sharing—Juvenile literature. [1. Sharing.]
I. Title. II. Title: Sharing. BJ1533.G4G65 1988
177'.7—dc19   88-35314
ISBN 0-86592-388-4

T 010064

Sharing

Do you know what **sharing** is?

Sharing is reading your sister one of your favorite books.

Sharing is giving money to charity so that someone who is hungry can eat.

When you let your best friend ride your bike, you're **sharing.**

Sharing is making popcorn for the whole family.

Hugs and kisses are meant to be **shared!**

Giving one of your favorite chocolate chip cookies to your friend is **sharing.**

Everyone is happy when the teacher **shares** a story with our class about Robin Hood.

Sharing is telling a friend about your secret place to be alone.

When you take turns using the tennis racket, that's **sharing.**

When you talk with your family about the things that happened at school or work, that's **sharing.**

When you and your brother do household chores, you're **sharing** family responsibilities.

Sharing is looking at a beautiful sunset with someone.

You're **sharing** when you talk with your friend because he's sad . . . **sharing** is caring.

Sharing is letting your friend play catch with your dog.

Sharing is telling someone special about your secret hopes and dreams.

Letting you brother borrow your crayons is **sharing.**

We **share** with others because it makes us feel good to make someone happy.

Sharing

Today was the day of the big parade. Jes and his dad were going to watch the floats and bands pass by.

"Come on, Dad. I'm ready," said Jes.

"Just a minute," yelled Jes's mom. "Take this umbrella. It may rain."

"Oh, Mom!" said Jes as he hopped into the car, picnic basket in hand.

"This parade is great, but I'm starved," said Jes. "Let's eat."

Just as he opened the picnic basket, there was a loud clap of thunder. Rain began to fall. Jes and his dad huddled under their umbrella.

"Those kids are getting soaked. "Get under my umbrella," Jes yelled to them.

Before long, four kids stood under the umbrella. They talked and giggled. Then they began to sing, "Rain, rain go away, Come again some other day."

How did **sharing** the umbrella make the parade more fun?

Tell about a time when you **shared** something special.

Sharing

"Achoo, achoo!" sneezed Kara. "I'm too sick to go trick or treating. Would you bring me some candy, Al?"

"I don't know. Maybe," said Kara's brother, Al. Then he hurried outside to join his friends.

By the end of the evening, Al's sack was so full of Halloween candy, he could hardly carry it home.

I'll eat my treats, so I won't have to share them with Kara, thought Al.

"Can I have some candy, Al?" asked Kara the next day.

Al didn't answer. He looked sick.

"What's wrong?" asked Kara.

"My stomach hurts—bad," said Al.

Just then Al's mom walked into his room carrying an empty sack.

"Al, don't tell me you ate all this Halloween candy!" she said.

What do you think would have happened if Al had **shared** his candy?

Why is it important to share with others?